ANNULMENT

A Step-by-Step Guide for Divorced Catholics

Rev. Ronald T. Smith

ASSISTING CHRISTIANS TO ACT

PUBLICATIONS

Chicago, Illinois 60640

ANNULMENT
A Step-by-Step Guide for Divorced Catholics
Rev. Ronald T. Smith

Edited by Thomas R. Artz
Cover design by Tom Wright
Typesetting by Garrison Publications

ACTA Publications
4848 N. Clark Street
Chicago, IL 60640
312-271-1030

Year 00 99 98
Printing 7 6 5 4
ISBN: 0-87946-127-6
Library of Congress Catalog Card Number: 95-078801
Printed in the United States of America

Table of Contents

To my parents and family,
with special thanks to Carol, Don and Dave,
who continue to encourage me
in my writings.

Introduction

Annulment: A Step-by-Step Guide for Divorced Catholics is written for those Catholics who have been divorced and who wish to marry again with the blessings of the Catholic Church. It is also written for those divorced Catholics who may not wish to remarry at this time, but who want to bring a greater degree of closure to their previous marriage.

This book will help you understand the annulment process and enable you to find healing, peace, and the strength to move forward with your life in a positive manner. Besides offering step-by-step instructions to help you complete the sometimes confusing annulment procedure, it also offers suggestions about restoring your relationship with your family, your friends, and your God.

Moreover, this practical guidebook will calm your fears about the annulment process, answer the most asked questions, and explain the annulment procedure and the options that are available to you.

Chapter one, "When Is a Marriage Not Really a Marriage," explains the conditions and qualities the Catholic Church expects to find in a valid sacramental marriage, and considers the difficulties and situations that indicate when what seemed on the surface to have been a Catholic marriage may not have been truly a sacramental marriage in the eyes of the Catholic Church.

"Who Needs an Annulment," the second chapter, explains who needs to obtain an annulment in order to be remarried in the Catholic Church, and how to begin the formal annulment process. It considers the appropriateness of the Catholic Church requiring such a procedure. It also provides suggestions on how to prepare yourself emotionally to take on the task of applying for an annulment.

The third chapter, "What Are the Steps in the Annulment Process," gives clear, concise, step-by-step directions for contacting the matrimonial tribunal, notifying the respondent (the former spouse), finding suitable affiants (witnesses), gathering the proper documents, filling out the data sheet, and writing the detailed history of the marriage.

The fourth chapter, "What Questions Must I Consider," provides a detailed list of questions to reflect on that will help you write the history of your marriage and prepare oral testimony about your marriage.

"What Happens at the Tribunal," the fifth chapter, explains the various stages your case will progress through once it has been delivered to the tribunal, the Catholic Church's court.

"What Should I Do if My Case Hits a Roadblock," the sixth chapter, examines more closely the options available if your case is closed before a hearing takes place or if an unfavorable decision is rendered.

"Can I Read a Sample Annulment Case," the seventh chapter, presents the complete text of several pertinent documents presented in an annulment petition. It gives the written testimony of the petitioner (the person seeking the annulment), the respondent (the other marital partner), and one of the affiants (witnesses). While this is a fictitious case, it contains details drawn from many marriages that ended in divorce. It is conditions like these that lead the Catholic marriage tribunal of a diocese or archdiocese to grant an annulment.

The final chapter, "How Can I Find Healing and Help to Begin Again," speaks to the heart and encourages ways to forgive oneself and move forward with hope and courage to enter new and healthy relationships.

There is also a glossary that explains and defines many of the complicated and technical terms that are used in the annulment process.

Although this book is written primarily for those applying for an annulment, respondents and witnesses as well as other family members may benefit from reading *Annulment: A Step-by-Step Guide for Divorced Catholics.*

This book is also a helpful resource for pastors, deacons, and pastoral associates involved in parish ministry. When presenting adult education classes or sacramental preparation programs, including the RCIA process, questions about marriage, divorce, and annulments often arise. This book offers clear, concise answers. The information in this book is also invaluable when talking with people who are registering in the parish or enrolling children in sacramental programs.

It is important to remember when applying for an annulment that *there are no guarantees that an annulment will be granted.* When the person seeking the annulment is aware of the many details of the process, when the information is presented in a logical fashion, when all the pertinent details are included in the testimony, and when the person perseveres to the end of the annulment process, it is more likely that a fair and honest decision will be rendered.

Annulment: A Step-by-Step Guide for Divorced Catholics will help you undertake and complete the annulment process in the best interest of all parties involved.

It is also designed to help you avoid the pain and confusion quite often associated with obtaining an annulment, so that it can truly become a healing process.

1. When Is a Marriage Not Really a Marriage?

The Catholic Church teaches that a valid sacramental marriage is a permanent, lifelong commitment between a man and a woman. In North America today, however, nearly half the marriages performed in the Catholic Church end in divorce.

What are the reasons some marriages succeed while others fail? Are some people more committed to their vows than others? How can a person know when it is okay to say, "It's time to end this unhappy union?"

It may be true that some people are more committed than others to making their marriage work, but the vast majority of couples approaching the altar truly have a strong desire to live the rest of their lives together. This is one reason there is so much pain and suffering associated with divorce.

When a marriage ends in divorce there is often a sense of personal failure. What was going to be so wonderful and blessed and happy becomes instead a terrible disappointment and a living hell. Love turns to hatred, dreams become nightmares. Confident, competent, loving people are transformed into scared, wounded, insecure individuals.

The Catholic Church for its entire two thousand year history has placed supreme importance on the permanent union of man and woman in marriage. Over time the Church has developed a criteria by which it judges the validity of marriages. In the eyes of the church a valid marriage is a union of a man and a woman who have the proper disposition and personality strengths to make a mature, lifelong commitment to a loving marital union that is permanent, exclusive, and open to children.

The Catholic Church expects marriages to last forever ("until death do us part") and thus does not recognize divorce or second marriages. At the same time, however, the Church realizes that some couples who get married are actually not capable of developing or maintaining a lifelong, loving union. The man and woman may have completed all the required preparations, have all good intentions, and have a beautiful wedding ceremony in a Catholic Church, yet still not have a valid marriage in the eyes of the Church. Upon further investigation, undertaken after the marriage has ended in divorce, it is determined that there was some radical defect, present at the start of the marriage and evident throughout the marriage, that rendered the marital consent inefficacious (that is, it did not produce the desired effect). When this is clearly and positively determined, the Church grants an annulment.

A decree of annulment does not say that a marriage ended in divorce. Rather, it says that, in the eyes of the Catholic Church, *a sacramental marriage never existed.* In other words, it is the belief of the Catholic Church that this couple was never married. Because the two people were not married, they are free to marry someone else in the Catholic Church.

Much confusion arises over the meaning of the annulment and its relationship to a civil divorce and to the legitimacy of the children that may have been born during the time the couple was considered married. There are several important points to keep in mind:

1. An annulment is a decree of the Church. It has no civil effect. Thus a person cannot begin the Church's annulment process until after he or she has been granted a civil divorce.

2. An annulment (also called a "decree of nullity") is a decree of the Catholic Church that a valid sacramental marriage did not exist between the two people. They may have lived as husband and wife for many years. They may even have had children, but in the eyes of the Church, they did not have a valid sacramental marriage.

3. When the Church grants an annulment *it does not render the children illegitimate*.

Before considering the annulment process and the criteria by which marriages are judged not to have existed, it is important to understand the conditions that the Church considers to be essential to a valid, sacramental marriage.

The Catholic bishops of the United States through their committee for pastoral research and practices clearly state what fosters the proper disposition and personality strengths needed for a sacramental marriage:

> A wise family training...leads children to discover...strengths and weaknesses....A gradual formation of the young person's character that, among other goals, instills esteem for all authentic human values, enhances skills in interpersonal and social relationships, develops an understanding and correct use of one's inclinations, and promotes a proper regard for and ability to mix with the opposite sex....Solid spiritual and catechetical training that pictures marriage and parenting as a true vocation and mission....
>
> *Faithful to Each Other Forever:*
> *A Catholic Handbook of Pastoral Help*
> *for Marriage Preparation*

The Church believes that two individuals, with the proper disposition and personality strengths, who have entered a marital relationship should be able to maintain a lifelong commitment to each other, through their own efforts and the grace of God. If one or both of these individuals do not have this required disposition or personal maturity, however, the marriage is usually doomed from the start.

Even in a valid sacramental marriage, the couple still encounters problems. No one is free of these. The couple needs to work together in resolving these conflicts by using their individual strengths and the grace of God. They must also be willing to seek help from other sources when necessary.

There are many things that can cause a union of a man and woman not to be a valid sacramental marriage. Annulments are granted when it is clear that the couple could not effect a mature, permanent marital relationship. The following are some of the situations that indicate a marriage may not be a valid sacramental marriage.

1. When one of the spouses is always responsible for the maintenance of the relationship and there is never a reasonable discussion of issues. Marriage is not meant to be one-sided.

2. When there is a history of substance abuse that had its origins before the start of the marriage and for which the individual refuses to seek help.

3. When there is a pattern of physical and verbal abuse and the offending person refuses counseling.

4. When there is a pattern of infidelity that indicates a person is incapable of maintaining an exclusive marital commitment.

5. When a person is completely closed to the possibility of having children. (Note that a couple does not have to have children to make their

marriage valid. This has nothing to do with a couple's ability or inability to have a child, but rather with their openness to parenthood.)

When one of these factors or a similar situation exists in a marriage, counseling of both parties is usually needed in order to resolve the problem. Every effort should be made to get both the husband and wife to participate in the counseling, but if this is impossible, there is value even when just one person seeks professional help.

A counselor, priest, or trained pastoral associate is able to take an objective look at the relationship from every side and evaluate whether the individuals have the necessary personality strengths to make the marriage work. Through the counseling, the parties can be assured they are trying everything possible to make the marriage work. With professional help the couple can come to a mature decision either to continue to work on the relationship, or to accept the fact that it is in the best interest of both individuals to end the marriage.

If the decision is made to end the marriage, either or both persons may desire to seek an annulment from the Catholic Church *after a civil divorce has been granted.* The remaining chapters of this book explain the annulment process and offer suggestions about completing it in a successful, healing manner.

2. Who Needs an Annulment?

- Who must go through the formal annulment process?

- Why does the Catholic Church insist that people go through the annulment process?

- Are long marriages or those involving children impossible to annul?

- With regard to civil law, will an annulment have an effect on the legal status of the children?

- How soon after a divorce should a person initiate an annulment?

- What does it cost to obtain an annulment?

These are just a few of the questions that are frequently asked by Catholics. This chapter will answer these questions and others that are raised by people whose marriages have ended in divorce or who are affected by someone else's divorce.

Many Catholics have the mistaken notion that all marriages that take place outside the jurisdiction of the Catholic Church are judged to be invalid in the eyes of the Church. This is not true. The Catholic Church recognizes and presumes the validity of all the following marriages:

1. Two Catholics married within a Catholic ceremony.

2. Two baptized non-Catholics married outside of a Catholic ceremony who have consummated their marriage.

3. A baptized Catholic, who converted to another religion and married a non-Catholic in a ceremony not sanctioned by the Catholic Church. (If the marriage took place before the promulgation of the 1983 Code of Canon Law, this marriage is invalid unless it falls into the category of number 4.)

4. A Catholic and a non-Catholic who were not married in a Catholic ceremony, but who had been granted a "dispensation from form": that is, the Catholic party had received permission from the Catholic Church to be married in a non-Catholic service.

Why does the Church require some non-Catholics to complete the annulment process?

Catholics who are planning to remarry (or who have remarried in a civil ceremony or in a ceremony at another church) and who wish to have their marriage recognized by the Catholic Church usually understand that they must complete the annulment process.

Many Catholics, however, who are planning remarriage or who are actually remarried but now want to be married in the Catholic Church, are unaware that their non-Catholic partner might also have to complete the annulment procedure. This regularly happens when the other individual is a non-Catholic Christian who was involved in one of the four marital situations described on page 16.

It may seem unfair that a non-Catholic is required to go through the Catholic Church's annulment procedure in order to marry a Catholic in the Catholic Church. The Church requires this, however, because it values the permanence and the sanctity of marriage between all couples, not just between Catholic Christians.

It should also be noted that when two people wish to be married and both individuals need to have a prior marriage annulled, many dioceses will not consider granting an annulment unless both parties apply for annulments from their prior marriages.

The annulment process can appear long and complicated. It can also seem to be an additional burden added to the feelings of frustration and anger that often accompany a failed marriage. Especially when people feel they were wronged by their former spouse, they can exclaim, "I don't know why I'm being punished. I wasn't the one who wanted the divorce. How can the Church be so unfair, preventing me from getting married again and being happy?"

There is little to be gained by a lengthy discussion about whether the Catholic Church has the right to require an annulment for anyone who wishes to marry again in a Catholic ceremony while a former spouse is still alive. It only causes a person to build up a wall of resentment, making it harder to complete all the work an annulment petition involves.

Rather than debating the fairness of the Church annulment requirements, a better question for an individual to ask is, "Am I emotionally ready to do all the required work in order to get this annulment?"

What about the children?

There is much misunderstanding about the effect of an annulment on marriages that endured for many years or produced children. There are people who believe it is impossible to annul such marriages. The Church does not agree. In the eyes of the Catholic Church, a marriage is not made valid by the number of years it exists or by the number of children it produces. A marriage is valid when two mature Christians enter into a permanent, monogamous union "for better or for worse, for richer or for poorer, in sickness and in health, until death do us part."

Since an annulment is a judgment solely of the Catholic Church, it is solely a spiritual matter. It has no civil effects on the children or the parties involved. This is one of the reasons a person must have obtained a civil divorce before the Catholic diocesan marriage tribunal will consider the case. The Catholic Church cannot annul a marriage that is still recognized as valid by a civil jurisdiction.

When should the annulment process begin?

With regard to the question of how soon after the divorce a person should apply for an annulment, the following points should be considered. While going through the annulment process, the person will have to examine his or her relationship to the former spouse. It is natural for the person to relive many of the painful experiences of the marriage; therefore, the individual may wish to wait a period of time before starting the annulment process. This gives the person an opportunity to emotionally recover from the relationship.

At the same time, a person does not want to wait too long to start the annulment process, since it will be necessary to find witnesses whose memories are still fresh enough to recall in detail the events of the now-ended courtship and marriage.

No matter when a person begins the annulment procedure, there will still be painful memories. One way to use these memories is to look at them as a learning experience. An individual's past experiences can assist a person in knowing what he or she wants and deserves in a future relationship. Looking at one's previous marriage helps to open a person's eyes to the things possibly overlooked in the past. Reviewing one's past honestly may indicate those areas in which change and growth are necessary for a healthier relationship with someone.

It is often a good idea to start the annulment process before entering deeply into a new relationship. It can take three months to two years or longer to complete the annulment process. Until an annulment is granted, it is impossible to set a date for a Catholic wedding ceremony. It is difficult to tell one's heart to be patient or to put one's life on hold for six months to a year, but it is necessary if a divorced person hopes to remarry in a Catholic ceremony. Applying for the annulment before another relationship develops and not setting a wedding date until the annulment is granted saves a great deal of emotional stress.

How much does an annulment cost?

Money cannot buy an annulment, and a lack of money does not deprive a person of obtaining an annulment.

Each diocesan tribunal sets its own fee for the annulment process. In effect, one does not pay for the annulment. Rather, one pays a sum (often between $250 and $2000) that helps to defray some of the costs of the tribunal office and its staff. In actual fact, the costs of running the office and paying the salaries of the tribunal staff far exceed the fee charged to the petitioner.

If a person cannot afford to pay the full fee, the tribunal may reduce the fee or waive it completely. Many tribunals also allow petitioners to pay the fee in installments.

The fee is assessed at the start of the proceedings and is the same whether the annulment is granted or denied.

Keeping all this in mind, the following chapter will consider the many steps involved in the annulment process.

3. What Are the Steps in the Annulment Process?

This chapter and the two following chapters will lead you step-by-step through the annulment process. Many people find the process to be complex and confusing. It can seem overwhelming when you add in the accompanying emotional pain and anxiety brought about by a divorce. Still, it is not impossible to obtain an annulment. Tens of thousands of annulments are granted each year in the United States and Canada alone and many more in other countries around the world—to ordinary people like you. You don't have to be a lawyer, a saint, a banker, a scholar, or a rich and famous person to receive an annulment. You simply have to be honest and to follow the guidance of the Church's diocesan officials. Their task is to assist you in this process and to see that justice is done while upholding the Catholic Church's belief about the sanctity and permanence of marriage.

Step One: Contact the Matrimonial Tribunal

The diocesan matrimonial tribunal is customarily located in its own office complex, but may also be located in an archdiocesan or diocesan office building. In a large archdiocese like Chicago or New York, dozens of priests, canon (church) lawyers, clergy, and lay staff members work full time on annulment cases in the marriage tribunal. In a smaller diocese a few individuals (priests, religious, and laity) may work part-time on annulment petitions. Either way, contacting this office is the best way to start your annulment process.

Your parish priest, pastoral associate, or deacon can give you the tribunal's address and telephone number. He or she can also explain the particular way that certain procedures take place in your diocese. This person can also assist you throughout the annulment process, both in completing the necessary forms and in finding the healing and peace you need to move forward with a hopeful spirit.

When calling the tribunal office, you should ask to speak to the secretary of the tribunal. The secretary is often the one who can best explain the requirements for petitioning the tribunal of that particular diocese. The tribunal may refer you (technically you are called "the petitioner") to someone on the staff of the marriage court who is located in your part of the diocese. On the other hand, you may be required to come into the office to start the annulment procedure. In some dioceses, information is sent through the mail so that you do not have to appear at the tribunal in person.

If the secretary mails you the information but does not give a referral to a member of the tribunal staff, ask the secretary to recommend someone in your area who can sit down with you and explain the information. If there is no one in the area, ask for the name of a person at the tribunal who can help if there are any problems or questions.

While most people undertake the annulment process in the diocese in which they are presently living, it is also perfectly acceptable to seek the annulment from the diocese in which one was married. This happens most often when someone has just moved to a new area after living for many years in another diocese. For more information on the proper diocese in which to file your annulment petition, see page 59.

Step Two: Notify Your Former Spouse

The tribunal has the obligation, whenever possible, to notify your former spouse (technically referred to as "the respondent") that it is examining his or her former marriage. In many cases it is to your advantage to contact your former spouse by telephone or by letter before you begin the annulment process. This helps to avoid some of the hostility your former spouse may feel if he or she is notified by the tribunal without prior warning that you have initiated a case before the matrimonial court. While you may not want to make contact with your former spouse, try to understand how you might feel upon receiving such notification without warning. Who would not prefer being notified in advance?

There are two reasons to be sensitive to the feelings of your former spouse. First, it is the right thing to do. Second, your annulment petition has a better chance of success if your former spouse cooperates with the process, especially if the information of the witnesses is weak.

You need not worry, however, about what will happen if your former spouse refuses to cooperate. Nearly all diocesan marriage tribunals are willing to consider an annulment petition even when the respondent (the former spouse) refuses to cooperate.

Step Three: Select Witnesses

The marriage tribunal normally asks you (the petitioner) to indicate two or more suitable witnesses or affiants. (Technically, witnesses give oral testimony and affiants submit written affidavits. In this book the two terms will be used interchangeably.) It is best to have both close friends and family members as witnesses. Having only friends and no family members as witnesses generally presents no problem. Unless it is absolutely necessary, however, it is best to avoid having only family members as witnesses. Family members are often a bit biased. Their insights into your relationship with your former spouse and with your family of origin are important, but when someone outside the family corroborates their statements, the insights will carry much more weight.

Some witnesses may be limited in their knowledge of you and your former spouse. People who only have information about your growing up years, or the years of your courtship, or the time of your marriage are not as valuable as people who have known you for a longer period of time. Testimony limited to one period of your life is not helpful when it is the only information that is offered. But when the tribunal receives testimony from a number of witnesses covering various periods of the petitioner's and respondent's lives, then this information becomes useful. Together, these testimonies can become equivalent to the testimony of a person who has known you or your former spouse for a longer period of time.

Although the tribunal may only ask for two witnesses, the tribunal does not restrict you from providing more. You should never coach the witnesses. When affidavits are received and are almost identical, grave suspicion falls upon the information, making the case harder to prove.

While you do not want to coach your witnesses, you can and should explain to them that the marriage tribunal is not asking them to provide a character reference for you. Rather, they should explain the problems that existed during your relationship with your former spouse (both during courtship and the years of your marriage). Encourage your witnesses to speak openly and honestly about the problems they observed in your marriage. The tribunal needs to know these problems in order to determine whether an annulment can be granted. Explain to them that speaking about someone's problems is not the same thing as saying the person is either bad or evil. Everyone has problems and the marriage tribunal wants to know the particular problems that occurred between you and your former spouse.

If your potential witnesses express hesitancy because they are not good writers or because they don't know where to start, you can put their minds at ease by telling them that most diocesan tribunals give them a series of questions to help them compose their answers. It's like a "fill-in-the-blanks" questionnaire. And assure them that tribunals don't grade for spelling or grammar. This is one time when it's the thought that counts.

Many witnesses are hesitant about providing confidential or personal information because they are fearful it will become public knowledge. In fact, many marriage tribunals in North America allow only the tribunal staff to read the information that is gathered. In most cases even the petitioner and respondent cannot read what the other person has written or what the witnesses have testified. Should witnesses be concerned about someone other than a tribunal official seeing their testimony, you should advise the witnesses to inform the tribunal that their affidavits or their testimonies are to be regarded as completely confidential. They should stress to the tribunal that no part of their affidavits or testimonies can be made public to anyone other than the members of the tribunal and its experts. If this cannot be agreed upon by the tribunal, then the individual may decide not to give any information.

If a witness agrees to answer the tribunal's questionnaire, you should stress the importance of completing it as soon as possible. The tribunal must often put a case aside for a long period while waiting for the testimony of the witnesses. A tribunal may send out reminders to the witnesses after a reasonable amount of time has passed, or it may notify you that an insufficient amount of information has been gathered and state what is needed for the case to continue. But this may not occur until several months after the questionnaires or outlines have been sent to the witnesses.

Because of the hundreds of cases the tribunal handles, there is always the possibility that an affidavit can get lost. Advise the witnesses to make a photocopy of their statements and offer to pay the cost of making those copies. The affidavits should be sent by certified mail so they can be traced if they are lost. Again, the petitioner should offer to pay the cost of the postage.

Step Four: Obtain the Required Documents

Another area that may slow down a case is gathering the required documents. Here is a list of the documents that are most often required and where a petitioner can obtain them:

1. Baptismal certificates (not birth certificates) of both the husband and wife, whether the baptism was at a Catholic, Protestant, or Orthodox Church. The parish that baptized the individual will provide the necessary certificate. The location of the respondent's baptism may be found in the Premarital Investigation Book of the parish where the marriage took place.

2. Marriage certificate (not the civil marriage license or civil certificate) obtained from the church where the marriage took place. Note, however, that the civil marriage license is needed when the marriage took place outside of the Catholic Church. A copy of this license can be obtained from the registrar of the town in which the marriage took place.

3. Final divorce decree. Normally, a person receives a copy of the final divorce decree at the time of the divorce. If not, the registrar of the town in which the divorce took place can provide one. Be sure the copy is readable. The tribunal must be able to find the following information on the divorce decree: the date, location, decree number, grounds, plaintiff's name, and custody agreement.

Step Five: Complete the Data Sheet

A data sheet is commonly attached to a written marital history. A data sheet provides information at a glance to the tribunal, allowing it to handle the case more quickly. Each tribunal has its own particular data sheet. Be sure to use its sheet. Here is the type of information normally required on a data sheet:

1. The petitioner's full name, maiden name if applicable, complete address (street, city, ZIP code), telephone numbers (both business and home), religion, date of birth, date and place of baptism.

2. The respondent's (former spouse) name,

maiden name if applicable, complete address (street, city, ZIP code), telephone numbers (both business and home), religion, date of birth, date and place of baptism.

3. The length of the courtship; that is, the period from when the couple met and started dating up to the time they were married.

4. The date the engagement took place. Note that whenever a date is requested, an exact date is ideal but an approximate date will do.

5. The date and place of the marriage.

6. The date of the final separation. Note that this is generally not the same as the date of filing for the divorce. The date of final separation is the date when the couple stopped living together in the same house or apartment.

7. The date and place of the divorce.

8. The names and dates of birth of the children if there are any.

9. A list of the petitioner's affiants or witnesses — title (Mr., Mrs., Ms., or Miss), full name, complete address and phone number, and your (the petitioner's) relationship to each person (that is, parent, brother, sister, relative, or friend).

10. A list of any professional counselors you and/ or your former spouse consulted. List their names, complete addresses, and the approximate dates during which the counseling took

place. Indicate counseling that took place before and after your marriage as well as during the time of the marriage.

11. Your present marital status and that of your former spouse. Did either of you remarry? If either has remarried, has the present spouse been married before? Was that person's first marriage annulled?

12. The outcome of any prior application for an annulment of this marriage or of a previous marriage, initiated by either spouse. The tribunal must know where and when this was done and what was the outcome of that annulment procedure.

13. Attach the documents mentioned in step four (baptism and marriage certificates and final divorce decree) to the data sheet.

Step Six: Write the Marital History

If the marriage tribunal requires a written marital history, keep in mind that you must paint a picture, in words, of the following areas: the background and family of origin of both you and your former spouse, your courtship, the day of the wedding, your honeymoon, your marriage from start to finish, and the present marital status of both of you.

Although the information sought is usually the same at each marriage tribunal, the questionnaire or outline may differ from diocese to diocese. It is best to follow the questionnaire or outline provided by your tribunal.

In writing a marital history (or an affidavit), never simply say, "yes" or "no." Always explain the answer fully in the written text. For example, if the question is, "Was there ever any unfaithfulness on the part of either?" do not simply answer, "Yes, there was unfaithfulness." The tribunal would need to know who was unfaithful, approximately when it took place, and how frequent it was.

Whenever possible give the approximate time frames (month and year) of any negative events. For example, the respondent may have been married prior to this marriage. The tribunal would need to know the approximate date of that marriage, the final separation, and divorce. Likewise if one party to the marriage developed a substance abuse problem, it is essential to give the progression of the problem noting its origin prior to the marriage and tracing its development throughout the marriage.

It is also important for the petitioner to provide examples of the issues. Examples paint a better picture. When a person describes someone as being immature, there can be many different interpretations of immaturity. With an example of immaturity, there is less room for misinterpretation.

Keep in mind while writing a marital history (or an affidavit), that the tribunal wants to know all the factors that contributed to the marital breakup so that it can decide if a true sacramental marriage ever existed. There is no need to give detailed examples of the positive aspects of the relationship. With regard to the negative aspects of the relationship, it is impossible to give too many examples.

One of the common mistakes often made by a petitioner is deciding the grounds for the annulment before writing the marital history. When a petitioner does this, the wrong grounds are usually picked and a lot of energy and time is spent describing the weakest grounds possible. It is better to write about all the issues in the relationship and to let the tribunal decide the grounds for granting the annulment.

Another common error occurs when the petitioner tries to write too brief a marital history, leaving out some of the most important information. It is better to write too much than too little. The tribunal can eliminate any unnecessary information, but it cannot create information that is not there.

When writing your marital history, try to state the facts objectively. Some petitioners make the mistake of trying to place the blame on someone, generally the former spouse. The annulment procedure is not designed to discover who is at fault but to decide whether a valid marriage contract ever existed. Trying to assign blame can divert one's attention from the problems that existed.

In writing the marital history, it is necessary at times to describe the problems, shortcomings, and failings of the petitioner, the respondent, and members of both families. This may cause you discomfort because from earliest childhood you have been trained not to speak badly about others. Often, because of this discomfort, the petitioner writes a marital history describing the perfect marriage. Remember that the tribunal is not in the business of annulling perfect marriages. It needs to know the problems of the relationship in order to grant an annulment.

There is nothing gained when you hold back a piece of information to prevent someone from thinking badly about you or about another person. If you are experiencing this temptation, it is helpful to remember that speaking about someone's problem is not the same thing as saying the person is bad or evil. He or she is simply a person with problems.

There is one other helpful hint to completing a marital history. Since writing it may be painful and may bring up old wounds that you would prefer to forget, it is easy to put off completing the marital history. To overcome this, give yourself a deadline in order to prevent procrastination.

The next chapter of this book offers questions that you can ponder as you write your marital history. They are intended to help you write a marital history that is accurate and complete, and that will increase your chances of receiving a positive decision regarding your annulment petition.

The fifth chapter explains the steps that occur after you have completed the marital history and presented it to the marriage tribunal.

4. What Questions Must I Consider?

Most diocesan marriage tribunals provide a list of questions to be answered or used as a guide when one completes the marital history portion of the testimony for an annulment. It is often the case, however, that the outline to be followed or the list of questions to be answered is not sufficiently detailed to help a person understand what information the tribunal is seeking.

The list of questions in this chapter is drawn from the questionnaires and outlines of many different marriage tribunals. It also includes the type of questions that are asked by tribunal officials in the course of their activities with people seeking annulments and with members of the tribunal staff.

The questions listed below provide a comprehensive outline of the areas about which the tribunal needs information in order to grant an annulment.

Before you write your marital history or testify as a witness, sit down with a pencil in hand and read through the list from start to finish. If a particular question stirs a memory, place a check mark next to it or make a brief note about the incidents it calls to mind.

After reading through these questions and noting the ones that are appropriate, you are ready to start writing your marital history. Using the form given to you by your marriage tribunal, address all the items or questions on the form, making sure to incorporate all the information and incidents that came to mind when you read through the extensive list of questions in this chapter.

If you are having difficulty understanding what is being asked by your tribunal in its outline or list of questions, refer back to this chapter and review the more detailed questions on the subject. When completing the tribunal's form, be sure that all the information recalled while reviewing the questions in this chapter has been incorporated into the proper segments of the marital history or affidavit that you are completing.

If you are required to have a personal interview with an official from the marriage tribunal, read through the questions several weeks before the interview. As you read the questions, make notes reminding you of the distant or forgotten memories triggered by the questions.

After going through the questions and recording the things that you had long forgotten and have just remembered, read through your notes several times until you feel comfortable remembering and talking about this information and the sometimes painful memories of the problems, difficulties, frustrations, and hurts of your past marriage.

The more complete your written and oral testimony and that of your witnesses, the better is your chance to receive a positive ruling in your annulment petition.

YOUR (PETITIONER'S) BACKGROUND

Mother:

1. Did your mother have any specific problems that caused tensions within the home, such as being verbally or physically abusive, misusing alcohol or drugs, or being chronically ill?

2. Was your mother a positive or a negative role model as a wife and a mother?

3. Were there any major problems between you and your mother while you were growing up?

Father:

1. Did your father have any specific problems that caused tensions within the home, such as being verbally or physically abusive, misusing alcohol or drugs, or being chronically ill?

2. Was your father a positive or a negative role model as a husband and a father?

3. Were there any major problems between you and your father while you were growing up?

Parents' Relationship:

1. Were there any major problems in your parents' marriage? If so, how did these affect your life?

2. If your parents are divorced, how old were you when the divorce took place? If custody was an issue, which parent received custody?

Stepparents:

1. If either parent remarried, did either stepparent have any specific problems that caused tensions within the home, such as being verbally or physically abusive, misusing either alcohol or drugs, or being chronically ill?

2. Were there any major problems in your relationship with your stepparent?

Brothers and Sisters:

1. How many brothers and how many sisters did you have? Did any of the brothers or sisters have any specific problems that would have caused tensions within the home, such as being verbally or physically abusive, misusing either alcohol or drugs, or being chronically ill?

2. Were there any major problems in your relationship with any of your brothers or sisters?

Family in General:

Were there any other specific problems that may not have been mentioned above, such as the divorces of other family members, serious illnesses or deaths, physical handicaps or emotional instability, or financial problems?

Education:

1. How much education did you receive?

2. If you did not complete high school, what year did you terminate your education and for what reason did you leave school?

3. If you attended college, what years did you attend? Did you live on campus? What degrees did you receive? If a degree program was not completed, what was the reason?

4. Did you experience any behavioral or serious personal problems during any of your school years or growing-up years?

5. In what type of social activities were you involved during your growing-up and school years?

Friendships:

1. Did you experience any difficulty in making friends?

2.   Were you more comfortable with casual friend-
     ships or with those of a deeper nature?

3.   What kind of reputations did your friends have?

Dating:

1.   Did you date much before you met the person
     you married (the respondent in these annulment
     proceedings)?

2.   Did you have any serious romances before fall-
     ing in love with your former spouse? If so,
     how long did it last, why did it end, and how
     soon after it ended did you meet your former
     spouse?

Military:

1.   Were you in the military service? If so, please
     give the years that were served and the rea-
     son for discharge.

2.   If your were in the military during your mar-
     riage, were there any times when you were
     separated from your former spouse for an ex-
     tended period? Indicate the length of time and
     its effect on your marriage.

Work History:

1.   During the time you were married, how many
     jobs did you have? If there was more than one,
     please provide the following information for
     each: the place of employment, the title of your

job, the length of employment, and the reason for leaving.

Mental Health:

If there is some question with regard to your mental health, please answer the following questions:

1. Were you ever treated for any type of mental health problem?

2. Has anyone ever hated you? Have you ever had a love/hate relationship with anyone? Did you ever feel someone was against you when there was no cause to feel this way?

3. If you acted irresponsibly during the marriage, was it the result of immaturity or an inability to be responsible?

4. Were your emotional responses appropriate for the circumstances you faced? Throughout your marriage, did you act on impulse or think things through carefully?

5. Do you have trouble telling the truth? Are you aware when you are lying? Would you lie even knowing there was a chance of being caught?

6. Do you have an ethical conscience, accepting guilt when it is appropriate?

7. During your marriage, were you able to think and act logically, without jumping from one topic to another?

8. Did you exhibit a tendency toward having anxiety attacks or thoughts of suicide? Were there extreme highs or extreme lows? If so, was there any pattern to the highs and the lows?

Physical Problems:

During your marriage were there any physical health problems, such as deafness, blindness, asthma, or cancer?

Fears:

Were there any fears that interfered with your life? Did you get married out of fear?

Goals:

What were your goals in life and in marriage? Were they realistic? How many of them were attained?

Religious Practice:

What was the nature of your religious practice before, during, and after the marriage?

Alcohol:

If there is a question with regard to the possible abuse of alcohol, please answer the following questions:

1. At what age did your drinking begin? Did it gradually increase over the years? Did the drink-

ing increase while facing difficulties? How heavy was it during the courtship, during the various stages of the marriage, and after the marriage? If possible, give examples when drinking adversely affected your life and your marriage.

2. Were you ever institutionalized for alcohol abuse? Did you join any organizations in an attempt to stop drinking alcohol? Did you ever try to stop drinking completely?

3. Did you ever have problems with pins and needles, trembling hands, ulcers, or any other physical symptoms associated with heavy drinking?

4. Did you ever have trouble paying attention, or experience hallucinations, loss of memory, amnesia or blackouts? Were you accident prone?

5. Did you ever become careless about your personal hygiene or personal appearance? Did your sense of responsibility deteriorate? Did drinking affect your employment?

6. While under the influence of alcohol were you ever paranoid, quarrelsome, jealous, cruel, or obscene?

Drugs:

If there is a question about your possible abuse of drugs, please answer the following questions:

1. When did you begin to abuse drugs? Were they prescription drugs or illegal drugs? What types of drugs were used? Did the intake of drugs gradually increase over the years? Did you use drugs more when faced with difficulties? How heavy was the drug use during your courtship, during the various stages of your marriage, and after the marriage?

2. Did you ever join an organization to help you stop the abuse of drugs? Were you ever institutionalized because of your abuse of drugs? Have you ever stopped using drugs completely?

3. Were there any physical side effects from the use of the drugs?

4. Did you have any trouble paying attention, or have any other mental health problems due to your use of drugs? Were you accident prone?

Gambling:

If there is a question with regard to gambling, please answer the following questions:

1. When did you begin to gamble? Did it gradually increase over the years? How heavy was your gambling during the courtship, during the various stages of the marriage, and after the marriage? At each of these stages, what was the least you bet and the most you ever bet?

2. Have you ever stopped gambling completely?

Traits:

1. Did you possess any of the following traits? If so, please state the trait or traits and provide an example of each: dishonest, excitable, fixer, gullible, impatient, inflexible, insensitive to others, irresponsible, jealous, loner, moody, naive, perfectionist, pessimistic, pleaser, possessive, quick tempered, selfish, self-righteous, shy, stubborn, suspicious of others, undependable, unethical, or a worrier.

2. What other personal traits had a negative effect on you or your relationship with your former spouse?

YOUR FORMER SPOUSE'S (RESPONDENT'S) BACKGROUND

Use the same set of questions that are given under "Your (Petitioner's) Background" (page 37) for your former spouse. Substitute "former spouse" for "you" ("respondent" for "petitioner") and answer the questions from the point of view of your former spouse.

COURTSHIP

First Meeting:

1. Where did you and your former spouse meet and under what circumstances?

2. What was the source of attraction between you and your former spouse?

Dating:

1. How often did you date—approximate number of times during the week? What type of dates did you have? What did you typically do and where did you go?

2. How much time did you have alone with each other—rarely, about average, more than average, or always? If rarely or always, please explain fully.

3. Was there premarital sexual intercourse? If so, how much was it a part of the relationship? Did it present a problem for either of you?

Communication:

1. Who customarily made the decisions on where to go, what to do, and with what friends to socialize?

2. Did either of you have much to say about the other person's lifestyle or friends: for instance, telling the other what type of clothing to wear or what friends were good or bad for them?

3. Was communication normally on an intimate level with the sharing of one's innermost feelings, or did communication remain at a surface level during the period of the courtship?

4. Did you discuss your values and beliefs about money, family, religion, and your future as a couple during the courtship? Did these values cause any conflict between the two of you?

5. Were there any serious arguments during your period of dating and courtship? If so, how often and how intense did they get? Was there any physical violence or verbal abuse?

Separations:

During your courtship were there any temporary separations? If so, please list the approximate date (month and year), the cause, the length of the separation, and the manner in which the relationship was resumed.

Engagement:

1. How did the subject of marriage arise? How did the engagement take place? Were you both happy about the engagement? How did your families feel about the engagement?

2. Who was involved with the wedding preparations? Were there any problems or disagreements in this area?

3. Did anyone advise you against the marriage? If so, please state who and the reason given for the advice.

Pressure:

1. Did anyone force either of you into the marriage? If so, please state who pressured you and how it was done.

2. Did either of you feel pressure to marry because of pregnancy, wedding preparations having been completed, threats, or embarrassment to your family if you did not get married?

3. Did either voice a reluctance to marry? If so, please provide the name or the names of those with whom you or your former spouse spoke.

Children:

1. How did each of you feel about having children? If either or both were against having children, please explain the reason or reasons why this was so.

2. Did either tell anyone that he or she had no intention of having children? If yes, please provide the name and address of anyone who knew this intention.

Fidelity:

1. How did each feel about faithfulness to one another during the marriage?

2. Was there any unfaithfulness during the courtship?

3. Does anyone have knowledge about you or your former spouse stating that he or she did not intend to be faithful during the marriage? If yes, please provide the name and address of anyone who knew of this intention.

Permanence of Marriage:

1. Did each of you view marriage as a lifelong commitment or was there a sense that this was a trial marriage that would be fine if it worked but that would be ended if it did not work out?

2. Did either of you see divorce as a viable solution to ending a problem marriage? If so, please explain under what circumstances the person saw this as permissible.

3. Before the marriage were there any conditions set on staying together during the marriage, such as providing there was no unfaithfulness?

4. Were you and your former spouse the type of people who made sacrifices?

WEDDING AND HONEYMOON

Rehearsal:

1. What were the attitudes of you and your former spouse during the rehearsal? Were there any unusual problems during this time? Were there any arguments?

2. What were the attitudes of each before arriving at the church or place of marriage? Were there any unusual problems? Was everyone on time? If not, who was late and why?

Church or Place of Marriage:

1. What were the attitudes of each of you at the church or place of marriage? Were there any unusual problems?

2. Did the family members on both sides come to the wedding? If not, who did not and why?

Reception:

1. What were the attitudes of each during the reception? Were there any unusual problems? Were there any arguments?

2. Did the petitioner and respondent stay together during the reception or were they seldom seen together?

Honeymoon:

1. What was the attitude of each during the honeymoon? Were there any unusual problems? Did you and your former spouse share common interests? Were there any arguments?

2. Was the marriage consummated during the honeymoon (that is, did you and your former spouse have sexual intercourse)? If not, was it consummated at a later time? When? If the marriage was not consummated during the honeymoon, then please explain the reason for waiting until a later time.

MARRIED LIFE

First Sign of Problems:

When (approximate year) did problems become obvious in your marriage? What were the issues?

Chores:

What was the attitude of each toward sharing the domestic chores? How was the division of chores accomplished?

Time Together:

1. What type of social life did you and your former spouse share? Was this an issue?

2. Did you spend much time alone together at home? If not, was this a problem? Also, when home together, how did you spend your time? Was there much interaction?

3. How intimate was the communication during the marriage? Did you share common interests and concerns? Did you discuss your differences without arguing? Were you able to resolve disagreements? Who regularly made major decisions?

4. Did you and your former spouse talk about your complaints with each other? If so, please list these complaints. Were they valid complaints?

Children:

1. If there were no children, was it an intentional decision or a physical problem with either of you? If intentional, was the decision mutually agreed upon? If intentional, how were children prevented?

2. If there were children, what was the attitude of each of you toward sharing in the childcare? How much quality time did each spend with the children?

Alcohol and Drugs:

1. Did the uses of alcohol have a negative effect on the marriage? If so, please provide some examples.

2. Did the uses of drugs have a negative effect on the marriage? If so, please provide some examples.

Violence:

1. Was there any physical violence on the part of either toward each other, the children, other people, the living quarters, or any other objects? If so, please provide examples and state the frequency of the violence.

2. Was there any emotional mistreatment on the part of either toward the other or toward the children? If so, please provide examples and state the frequency of the emotional abuse.

Sexual Activity:

1. What was the attitude of each in regard to genital sexual activity during the entire marriage? How were differences in sexual practices, preferences, and sensitivities addressed?

2. Were both satisfied with the frequency of sexual intercourse? Were there any desires of either that were thought to be perverted or out of the ordinary?

3. In your marriage, who regularly initiated sexual relations? Was either party ever unwilling to participate? Was foreplay prolonged?

4. Were both you and your former spouse able to reach an orgasm? If not, was there any evidence that the person would have been able to do so with a different partner?

Sexual Dysfunction:

If there is a question as to how knowledgeable you or your former spouse were on matters of sexuality or if there was serious sexual dysfunction, please answer the following questions with regard to that person only:

1. Was there an awareness that one of the main purposes of marriage was to have children? Was there a clear understanding of the reproductive system of the man and woman?

2. Was it ever necessary to seek professional advice either by counseling, by books, or by articles because of a feeling of ignorance about sexual matters?

3. When sexual intercourse was attempted for the first time, were there any problems?

4. If the first experience of sexual intercourse was unpleasant for either spouse, did it ever become a pleasurable experience later in the marriage?

Homosexuality or Lesbianism:

If there is some question with regard to the sexual orientation of you or your former spouse, please answer the following questions with regard to that person only:

1. When did it seem that there might be some question as to the person's sexual orientation?

2. Were there ever any sexual relations with anyone of the same sex? If so, when did this occur and how often?

3. Was the individual more comfortable with the opposite sex or with the same sex?

4. Would the person be willing to change his or her sexual orientation?

Infidelity:

1. Was there any unfaithfulness on the part of either? If so, please provide the approximate dates for when the infidelity started and stopped, and whether there was more than one affair.

2. Did you or your former spouse subsequently marry any of these people?

In-laws:

Did either have a serious problem with the in-laws?

Finances:

1. Was gambling an issue during the marriage? If yes, please explain how heavy the gambling was during the different stages of the courtship and marriage.

2. Were there any difficulties in the area of finances? If so, please explain. If it was due to foolish spending, please state by whom and on what the money was spent. How much in debt were the petitioner and respondent at the time of the final separation?

Housing:

1. Were there any problems with the type of housing? Were there any problems with the location of the residence?

2. Were the living quarters shared by more than one family?

Temporary Separations:

Were there any temporary separations? If so, please indicate for each separation the approximate date (month and year), the length, the cause of the separation, and the reason for reconciling.

Final Separation:

1. What was the cause of the final separation?

2. Who left the house or apartment?

3. Were there any attempts at reconciliation after the final separation? If yes, please explain what happened.

Counseling:

Did either you or your former spouse receive any counseling? If so, please provide the following information for each counselor: name, address (institution, street address, city, state and ZIP code), the approximate dates of the counseling (month and year), and whether one or both parties attended the counseling sessions.

PRESENT STATUS

You (Petitioner):

1. Have you remarried? If yes, what was the status of your present spouse at the time of the marriage: single, divorced, or widowed?

2. If you are remarried, what is the status of this present marriage? Has this union produced any children?

3. If you had children with your former spouse and custody was granted to your former spouse, do you visit the children? If not, please explain.

4. If you are required to pay child support, is it up-to-date? If not, what is the reason?

5. How is your life progressing? Are there any major problems?

YOUR FORMER SPOUSE (RESPONDENT)

Use the same five questions listed under "You (Petitioner)," substituting "your former spouse" for "you" in the five questions.

By reviewing and answering these questions patiently, truthfully, and completely, you will be well on the way both to healing from your past marriage and to presenting the strongest possible case for an annulment.

For an example of a complete marital history based on the questions presented in this chapter, please refer to chapter seven.

5. What Happens at the Tribunal?

It is not necessary to know every detail of the tribunal procedures in order to obtain an annulment, but it is helpful to understand some of the basic activities that take place. This chapter will start by explaining the procedure for delivering one's petition to the tribunal and will continue through all the steps taken en route to the rendering of a decision regarding the petition for an annulment.

The steps outlined in this chapter follow immediately from the six steps explained in chapter three of this book.

Step Seven: Deliver the Marital History to the Tribunal

Once the marital history is completed, it should be given to the secretary of the tribunal, along with the completed data sheet and documents. There are several ways in which this can be accomplished. It can be sent by way of the local parish priest, but this is inadvisable. A parish priest seldom has cause to be at the tribunal or at the chancery office; therefore, the case can sit on his desk for a few months. A better way is to send the marital history by certified mail directly to the secretary of the tribunal. Several days after mailing the marital history, the petitioner should check with the tribunal office to see if all the information has been received.

The third, and safest way, is to hand deliver all the documents to the secretary of the tribunal. The petitioner avoids the agony of wondering whether the material arrived safely. Also, by quickly reviewing the materials when you deliver them, the secretary of the tribunal can inform you if there is anything missing or if something else needs to be done in order to speed up the handling of the case.

Be sure to make photocopies of all the documents and of the marital history.

Step Eight: Establish Competence

After the tribunal receives your marital history or your initial request to consider the case, it is necessary to establish competence. In simple language, the marital tribunal needs to make sure that it has the jurisdiction to hear the case.

There are four grounds on which a tribunal may base its competence to decide the annulment petition:

1. If the marriage took place in this diocese;

2. If your former spouse (the respondent) lives in this diocese;

3. If you (the petitioner) currently live in the diocese;

4. If most of the proof can be found in this diocese.

Although the first two grounds take precedence over the last two, it is possible for your former spouse's tribunal to grant permission for you (the petitioner) to present the annulment petition to another tribunal as noted in points three and four.

Step Nine: Initial Review of the Case

With competence established, the tribunal performs an initial review of the case. This may be done by a judge of the marriage tribunal, the secretary, or another member of the staff who has been delegated to perform this task.

It is at this stage that weak cases are weeded out. On occasion, but not often, you (the petitioner) may be urged to withdraw the case until better evidence can be established, thereby making it easier to reopen later.

Step Ten: Contact the Parties Involved

If it appears that a solid case is likely to be developed in support of the annulment petition, you (the petitioner) are usually requested to sign a "formal petition form" and to supply any missing documents.

If you have used the services of a professional counselor, you will be asked to sign a release form so that the tribunal can obtain any available records that will aid in understanding more clearly the issues that led to the failure of the marriage.

Once the tribunal receives the signed petition form and the petition is accepted by a judge, the tribunal contacts the witnesses. Each witness is sent either a questionnaire or an outline of the types of information being sought.

Although the majority of tribunals do this through the mail, some require oral testimony; therefore, appointments may be scheduled for the witnesses at this point.

If you wish to keep on top of the case and insure that it moves along swiftly, it is a good idea to contact the tribunal a month after sending in the signed petition form. Call the tribunal to see if the witnesses were notified and whether they have responded.

If the tribunal notified the affiants but an affidavit or two is missing, contact the witnesses whose affidavits are missing and encourage them to send in their responses.

While checking with a witness, you may find that the affidavit was already sent. The affidavit may have been lost either in the mail or at the tribunal office. Ask the witness to make another copy of the original testimony and send it to the tribunal via certified mail. Offering to pay for the copying and the postage is both a polite gesture and a way to speed the process along.

If the witness has not responded, it may be because he or she finds it too difficult to write about the problems that led to the breakup of the marriage. After you have spoken to the witness a few times, you are best not to push any further. Accept the fact that the witness will not be responding and send the tribunal the name and address of another witness. Why lose a friend or hurt a family relationship by forcing someone to complete an unpleasant task?

With the acceptance of the petition, the tribunal contacts the respondent (your former spouse) to provide him or her an opportunity to cooperate with the case and provide information and recollections from his or her point of view.

The respondent is given a reasonable amount of time to state his or her intention with regard to cooperating. The average time given is about three months. If your former spouse does not respond within this length of time, the tribunal assumes the respondent's decision is not to respond and continues the case based on the information it has obtained from you (the petitioner) and the witnesses.

Step Eleven: The Second Review

After the tribunal receives a sufficient number of affidavits or testimonies, and possibly hears from the respondent, another review is done in order to establish the grounds for the case. After reviewing the case, it may decide more information is necessary before establishing the grounds. In that case you may be asked to expand certain areas of the marital history or the witnesses may be asked additional questions.

Step Twelve: Preparing the Presentation

As soon as the grounds are established, the case is put on a waiting list for assignment to a member of the tribunal staff who will prepare the case for a presentation. The length of time it takes a case to be assigned depends greatly upon the backlog at the tribunal. The range is wide, from three to fifteen months, depending on the number of petitions submitted and the size of the staff at the particular diocesan marriage tribunal.

When the preparator (the person who gathers all the information and presents the evidence) receives a case, he or she reads through the marital history, the respondent's affidavit (if one was sent in) and the affidavits of the witnesses. After studying the evidence, the preparator may decide to question further the parties involved either by correspondence or personal interview. It is also the preparator's responsibility to interview the respondent if he or she has requested one. The interview of the respondent may take place either before or after the interview with the petitioner.

It is often helpful if you release the preparator from the need to maintain confidentiality in regard to the marital history you submitted. If you do this, the preparator can confront the respondent (your former spouse) when major conflicts become obvious regarding the facts of the case. If the preparator is restricted by confidentiality from disclosing what he or she has learned from studying the marital history you prepared, it will be necessary to get back in touch with the petitioner in order to receive permission to confront the respondent with the petitioner's point of view on particular issues. After permission is granted, contact with the respondent must be re-established. This is time consuming and can be avoided if the preparator is released in advance from confidentiality regarding the petitioner's marital history.

Fear that the preparator will tell the respondent too many details of the marital history you have prepared may cause you to hesitate releasing the preparator from confidentiality. To remove this fear, you should insist that the only part of the marital history that may be made know to the respondent is the part in which major conflicts exist. This leaves little room for misunderstanding by the preparator.

Although the preparator may not need any additional information, it is normal to meet with you at least once before the presentation of the case, unless this is impossible because of distance. During the interview with the petitioner, the preparator may ask a few more questions to clarify a point or two. Generally, this session will not involve many new questions. This interview is also an opportunity for the preparator to meet the petitioner and to answer any questions you might have about the procedure.

There are two questions, however, that the preparator is unable to answer during this appointment. Quite understandably, you want to know, "How strong or how weak is my case?" This is a difficult question for the preparator to answer since he or she is not the judge. You can ask the question but don't expect the preparator to volunteer much information.

The second unanswerable question is, "How much longer will this take?" Most preparators are cautious about giving a time for completion because the case still must proceed through several stages, and at any stage the tribunal may want a deeper investigation, which will cause a delay. Across the USA and Canada, on occasion some tribunals render decisions in three months; others routinely take two years or more to decide an annulment case. It is best to start the annulment process as soon as possible and not to set a wedding date until the final decree of nullity is in hand.

Generally nothing else is required of the petitioner after the personal interview. On rare occasions, however, a judge may request to see a petitioner or may ask the preparator to recontact the petitioner in order to clarify a particular issue. Once the preparator feels all the available information is gathered, he or she will seek permission to present the case before the first instance court. Permission is usually granted. If permission is denied, the only way to continue the case is either to supply new and stronger evidence or establish new grounds. If neither is available, the case is usually closed, but this should not be interpreted as a "negative decision" being rendered. The procedure to reopen a case involving a "negative decision" will be discussed in chapter six.

Step Thirteen: Presentation Before the First Instance Court

When permission to present a case is granted, the preparator requests a date to appear before the first instance court of the tribunal. The number of people present at the hearing varies from one diocese to another. The court is customarily composed of the judge, the defender of the bond (whose job it is to argue that the marriage was indeed a valid marriage in the eyes of the Church when evidence supports such a claim), the preparator, and one or more experts (for instance, a psychologist, counselor, canon lawyer, or pastor).

The petitioner, respondent, and witnesses are not usually present when a case involves a written marital history and affidavits. When oral testimony is being used, a tribunal might require some or all of the parties involved to be present at the hearing.

The preparator makes the presentation of the evidence to the court. A discussion follows. If the judge, after hearing all the evidence and the opinions of the various members of the court, feels there is sufficient evidence to render a decision granting an annulment (also called a "declaration of nullity"), the judge will do so.

If the judge does not feel there is sufficient evidence to render a decision, the judge may have the preparator recontact some or all of the parties in order to obtain some specific information related to certain matters in the case.

If the judge is of the opinion that continuing the investigation would not be beneficial, he or she will either render a "negative decision" or an "informal negative" (also known as "withholding a decision").

When the first instance court renders an affirmative decision, someone from the marriage tribunal will notify you (the petitioner) of the court's decision. Most often this is done by letter. It will explain, however, that before the final declaration of nullity is granted, the appellate court must hear the case.

Step Fourteen: The Appellate Court Review

At this point you can begin to relax since the appellate court upholds most first court decisions. In most tribunals less than fifteen percent of the decisions are overturned by the appellate court.

Should the appellate court overturn an affirmative decision of the first court, it will render either a "negative decision" or an "informal negative."

When the appellate court upholds the decision of the first instance court, the petitioner and respondent are both notified of the decision by the tribunal. Provided the tribunal places no prohibition on either the petitioner or the respondent, and their future or present spouses have no previous marriages needing to be annulled, the petitioner and respondent are free to proceed with wedding plans in the Catholic Church.

The letter from the tribunal office should be sufficient to prove the person is free to marry.

Step Fifteen: A Prohibition to Remarry

When the circumstances of the case warrant it, a tribunal may prohibit an individual petitioner or respondent from marrying in the Catholic Church. This is done when the tribunal feels that the person is incapable (either temporarily or permanently) of establishing and maintaining a valid Catholic marriage.

If the prohibition is temporary (pending counseling, treatment, rehabilitation, or the like), it is necessary to remove the prohibition before a Catholic wedding ceremony can take place.

Only the person who has the prohibition is prevented from marrying within the Catholic Church. The person without the prohibition is free to set a date to marry immediately.

6. What Should I Do if My Case Hits a Roadblock?

Is it difficult to get an annulment? That depends on how you look at the results.

Many people begin the annulment process but then give up along the way. They either don't complete the marital history, don't provide the names of witnesses, or don't return phone calls and letters from the marriage tribunal asking for more information. The case remains open indefinitely but is never brought to completion for lack of necessary documentation or testimony. Of course, these people are not granted an annulment.

The news is much better for people who complete all the steps in the annulment process. In the United States and Canada, the vast majority of annulment petitions are granted a favorable ruling. If you complete all the forms, prepare a sound marital history, select helpful witnesses who also complete the necessary affidavits and respond to all the inquiries and requests for further information from the marriage tribunal, you have a very good chance of being granted an annulment.

There are occasions, however, when a case runs into a roadblock and receives either a "negative decision" or an "informal negative."

When this happens the case may be reopened either by acquiring stronger evidence or by considering new grounds on which to base the petition for annulment. When new grounds are established it is usually due to new information being gathered or uncovered.

There are a number of ways to gather new information. If the respondent (former spouse) did not give testimony, it may be worthwhile to contact your former spouse again to see if he or she is willing to reconsider. You have nothing to lose by trying once again to gain the respondent's cooperation.

Additional testimony from the witnesses who have already testified can be another source of new information. Talk with your witnesses to see if they have more to offer. A personal interview by a member of the tribunal staff often proves to be beneficial as it raises issues that the witness might not have mentioned in previous written or oral testimony.

Although the witnesses named by the petitioner and respondent are always contacted, they do not always reply. Contact the people who have not replied to see if they are willing to reconsider.

It is also possible to identify new witnesses. If this is necessary, review the recommendations in Step Three: Select Witnesses on page 25.

Whenever there are new sources of information, the tribunal should be notified of this and asked to re-open the case. Most tribunals will agree to this although some require that the case be started all over from the beginning. Either way, it is more hopeful than a negative decision.

The key to restarting a case or gaining a review is the inclusion of additional evidence. Without new evidence or someone new coming forth to give an affidavit or new testimony, there is little that can be done.

There is one other option, although it is a bit extreme. When a case is closed without a hearing or without a decision being rendered, the petitioner can insist upon a hearing in the first instance court and the rendering of a decision. If the decision is negative, which is normal under those circumstances when no new evidence has been presented, then the petitioner can appeal the decision either to the appellate court or to the Rota (the Catholic Church's highest tribunal located in the Vatican).

If you receive a negative decision, either from the appellate court or the Rota, however, the decision is usually final and cannot be appealed under ordinary circumstances. It also should be noted that an appeal to the Rota, however, is quite time-consuming and regularly ends in a negative decision.

7. Can I Read a Sample Annulment Case?

Your diocesan marriage tribunal will give you an outline to follow or a set of questions to answer in preparing your marital history. Your former spouse, if he or she agrees to cooperate, will receive a similar outline or set of questions. Each witness will also receive an outline or series of questions to guide his or her testimony.

If you are preparing a written response—and diocesan tribunals use written responses more often than personal interviews—be thorough and complete, even if it means writing or typing ten or fifteen pages or more.

Marriage tribunals are concerned about the facts and events. They overlook grammar and spelling errors, but if you have trouble putting your thoughts in writing, it is okay to ask a trusted friend or relative for help. One man who did not have much formal education and who rarely had to write more than his signature, asked a friend who was a stenographer to transcribe his answers to the questions in the same way she would turn her boss's dictation into a business letter or report. He talked, she typed, and the result was a complete, accurate marital history that resulted in his receiving the annulment he sought.

The following examples as well as the names, places, and events are completely fictitious in nature, although they are based on actual facts. Although only one witness's affidavit is given here, tribunals almost always obtain testimony from several witnesses.

As you will quickly see, the petitioner and respondent's view of the relationship can be quite different. This is the reason there is a need for knowledgeable witnesses from both parties, plus the need for the petitioner to release the preparator from strict confidentiality, so that he or she can better determine for the marriage tribunal what actually took place when the testimony of the former husband and wife does not agree.

The testimony that follows is presented by:

Carol Shield: The Petitioner
Thaddeus Jones: The Respondent
Roberta Stowe: The Witness

PETITIONER'S MARITAL HISTORY

Carol's Background:

My mother was a good hearted person who

had the patience of a saint. I was very close to her because she used me as her confidant.

My father was a heavy drinker who became physically violent when he was intoxicated. On many nights there were intense arguments, with my father physically abusing my mother. The arguments were so violent I feared for my mother's life. Although my father never physically abused any of the children, emotionally he nearly destroyed us all. He criticized everything anyone did.

Because of my father's nature, I was not close to him, and at times I hated him because of what he did to my mother. I looked forward to the day I could get away from him.

I am close to my two sisters and one brother. My brother is single. Both of my sisters are divorced and have not remarried.

Another source of tension within the home was financial, caused by my father's drinking. I had to lie many times to bill collectors who were looking for my parents. This caused me a great deal of guilt. Because of these financial problems, I was unable to attend college, completing only four years of high school.

I did not make friends easily because of being shy. The friends I had, I never brought home, because I never knew how my father would be. There were times when he embarrassed me in front of my friends.

I was not allowed to date until my senior year of high school and Thad (my former husband) was my first date. I never dated anyone else.

With regard to my work history, other than part-time jobs, I was a full-time wife and mother during my twenty-five years of marriage. Thad wanted me to stay home with the children, even though we had financial problems throughout the marriage.

I have never had any mental health problems. The only fear I had was the fear of my father.

My goals in life were to have a happy marriage, healthy children, and a good job.

I practiced my religion faithfully.

I never abused drugs or alcohol. I never had any problems with handling money, except that we didn't have much. I never gambled, other than a dollar lottery ticket now and then.

I see my strengths as being a good listener and having a willingness to help others. I am sensitive to the needs of others, and I enjoy making people happy.

My weaknesses include being a perfectionist—very demanding of myself and others;

moody—whenever things seem to be going wrong, I find myself getting depressed; and being suspicious of others—it takes a lot for me to trust people; perhaps, I still don't trust anyone, other than God.

Thaddeus' Background:

He seldom talked about his family. His mother seemed moody, cold, and domineering. She always wanted to know what everyone else was doing. She was extremely harsh on the children, using a belt in disciplining them while they were growing up.

Thad's father was a passive man and a heavy drinker who usually fell asleep each evening with a beer in his hand. Unlike my father, Thad's father was never violent. His parents seemed to love one another, but they made few outward signs of affection toward each other or the children. His mother was definitely the boss. His parents didn't seem to have much of a social life.

Thad's relationship with his parents was a strange one. He felt his father was spineless and his mother was a witch. During his high school years, Thad became rebellious. One day, when his mother was beating him with the belt, he pushed her to the floor, took the belt, then threatened to beat her to death if she ever touched him again. She never did.

Thad was close to his brother, who was his drinking buddy. They would go bar hopping quite often. His brother never married, remaining at home with his parents. There were no financial problems within his family since his mother came from a wealthy family. I am not aware of any divorces within his family, other than ours.

During high school, Thad was often involved with fights, skipped school frequently, and had bad grades. He had no desire to go on to college because he was working at his father's auto body shop and was making good money. His only friends were his drinking buddies and his brother. Thad used to buy rounds for all his drinking buddies. I was the only girl he ever dated.

Thad did not enter the military service. His work history was actually quite good, always working for his father's auto body shop. He never missed a day, even if he was sick from drinking the night before. He had no specific mental health problem other than his violent temper, which was a result of his drinking. He feared no one!

Thad never spoke of any goals and never shared any with me. He seemed to live from day to day.

He never practiced his Catholic religion, except on holidays like Christmas.

Thad had a definite problem with alcohol. He drank from the time I first saw him. During the courtship, he was only a beer drinker.

He would have maybe two or three beers whenever he drank, usually on weekends. Later in the marriage, he got into the hard alcohol, drinking maybe a pint to a quart of Canadian Club a day. He never tried to stopped drinking because according to him he didn't have a problem. When drinking, he would jump from one topic to another. There would be times when he would lose his temper violently. I explain this in greater detail under the marriage section.

After a night of drinking, he would wake up and not remember how he got home. He became very careless about his personal hygiene, not bathing for days at a time, not even showering.

He was extremely jealous, constantly accusing me of being unfaithful both during the courtship and the marriage. In fact, I was always faithful to him.

He never talked about any physical problems, other than having a lot of gas.

He did not abuse drugs and had no problem with gambling.

Thad's strengths are his good sense of humor and the fact that he would do anything for a friend (but not for his family). He went to work every day, and that was another strength.

His weaknesses centered around his drinking: insensitive to my emotional needs, bad temper, jealousy, and possessiveness. Both during the courtship and the marriage, he checked on me daily by telephone to be sure I was where I said I would be.

Courtship:

We met during our senior year of high school. Thad started to call every day and he even visited the house from time to time. I was physically attracted to him, plus I enjoyed the attention that he showed me. I thought his possessiveness was love.

We dated about twice a week, mostly on Fridays and Saturdays. We took walks, visited with friends, went to movies, and had drinks with the guys. He usually made the decisions on what we were going to do and with whom.

He never wanted me to go out with my friends or even with my family. Whenever he saw me talking to any boys in school, he would accuse me of being unfaithful to him, get furious, and threaten to break off the relationship. He told me I would never find someone who loved me as much as he did. I believed him. We never had any deep discussions; we only talked about his friends and about how much I hated my father and wanted to get out on my own.

After about six months of dating, we were at a drive-in movie when he convinced me to have sex with him as a sign of my love. I became pregnant that evening. When we discovered this, we decided the only right thing to do was to get married and give the child a name. Although we had not discussed marriage until this time, we did love one another. It was also a perfect opportunity for me to get out on my own and away from my father.

We were happy about the idea of becoming parents. We both believed in the importance of fidelity, and we didn't believe in divorce at the time. There were no temporary breaks during the courtship. Both families agreed it was the proper thing to do and very little preparation went into getting married.

Only our parish priest cautioned us about getting married so quickly. The priest suggested we wait until after the child was born, but I couldn't think of doing this since my father was being verbally abusive about my pregnancy and calling me a slut who shamed the whole family. I had to get out of the house.

Wedding and Honeymoon:

We had no problems on the night of the rehearsal, except that afterward Thad drank a little more beer than he usually did. It was a small wedding, with no unusual problems at the church. For a reception, we had a meal at a restaurant with his parents, my parents, the best man and maid of honor. His mother and my father had an argument over whether it was Thad's or my fault that I got pregnant. We had no honeymoon because we had no money.

Married Life:

We were married for twenty-five years and had four children. During the marriage, we always had our own apartment, but not always in the nicest part of town. At least it was our own, not my father's or his mother's. Thad never helped in household chores or with childcare. This was totally my responsibility. Thad said he was the bread winner and that was his only responsibility. Although he earned good money, I would not call him a good bread winner since he spent a lot of money on drinking, making it impossible to save any money.

Within the first year of marriage, problems began with his going out almost nightly to be with his brother. They went drinking usually. Whenever I questioned him as to where he was going, he would tell me to mind my own business. On the nights he stayed home, he fell asleep on the couch watching TV and ignoring me. The only social life that I had was talking on the telephone or visiting my friend, Roberta Stowe. At times, when Thad was out, she would visit me. Roberta was a great support to me throughout the marriage.

Communication was poor between us. I would try to talk to him about the kids, but he told me not to bother him with their problems.

Whenever I forced any issues, especially if he had been drinking, he would smash lamps, dishes, and whatever was around. There were numerous pictures hung over holes in the wall. As the marriage progressed, the drinking got more intense and so did the violence. He started to knock me around, even once when I was pregnant with our third child.

This was during 1972. While beating me, he would say I deserved it because I drove him crazy. I got to the point that I believed him. He said I could leave anytime, but that no one would ever want me. He told me that I was a lousy mother and that he would get the kids if we split up. He really convinced me so I stayed with him.

The only drug abuse was the alcohol abuse. Our sex life was repulsive to me for two reasons: he smelled because he didn't bathe, and he used to force himself upon me when I was reluctant. I am not aware of any unfaithfulness on his part, and there was definitely none on my part.

His mother constantly questioned me with regard to whether Thad was happily married. His mother said if he wasn't, he could always return home. I never told her about his violent temper, but I did tell her that he drank heavily. She said he deserved to go out for a drink after working hard all day.

My parents felt I made my bed; therefore, I had to lie in it. For the sake of the kids, I felt the same way.

We had no temporary separations, because I always feared losing my children. I did try to get him to see a marriage counselor or a priest with me. He said he was happy with the way things were and that I was the one with a problem, not him.

Final Separation:

Each of the children when they turned eighteen left the house and went off on their own. I had only one child left at home. One evening, my daughter, who was sixteen at the time, got into an argument with Thad. He punched her squarely in the face, knocking her out. I thought he had killed her.

Right then and there, I knew I could never stay with him and risk having her injured again by him. Once my daughter became conscious, I took her and went to Roberta's. She let us stay until I found my own apartment.

Present Status:

I am presently working as a secretary for a law firm. I hope to return to school in order to get a better position. I am dating, but nothing serious at the present time.

Thad doesn't have to pay child support because my youngest child is no longer a minor. He keeps in touch with the children sporadically. I have no contact with him. The children tell me that he has returned to his parents' home and is still drinking as heavily as ever, but still denies having any problem with alcohol. With regard to any romantic involvement, I do not know if he has any.

RESPONDENT'S AFFIDAVIT

Thaddeus' Background:

My relationship with my family is good and my brother is my best friend. My parents have a good relationship. There were no unusual problems within my family. I never enjoyed school that much. I looked forward to working at my father's auto body shop full-time. I have always worked for him and have never missed a day of work. I have a lot of friends.

I never dated until I met Carol.

I never served in the military. I have no mental health problems or physical problems. I can honestly say I fear nothing.

My goal in life is to own my father's business and to be happily married. I stopped attending church when my parents did while I was in grammar school.

I definitely have no problems with alcohol or with drugs. I might have a few drinks at the bar with my friends to unwind after work, but I never drink more than they do. People who use drugs are stupid. I never gambled, other than the state lottery.

My strengths are being helpful, having a good sense of humor, being a hard worker, and a good provider. Other than giving in too easily, I really can't think of any weaknesses that I have.

Carol's Background:

Carol said that her parents didn't get along too well because of her father's drinking, but I never thought he drank that much. Carol was close to her mother, but not to her father. She almost feared him, but I never asked why. She seemed to get along with her brother and sisters. She was a high school graduate but never went to college.

I believe I was the first person she dated. She never served in the military. She never worked a full-time job because she had the responsibility of taking care of the kids during the marriage. She had no mental health problems or physical problems, and she had no fears.

We never spoke about setting any goals. She went to church weekly with the kids.

The only problem she had with alcohol was

that she thought anyone who drank had a problem with alcohol. She used to drive me crazy with this. She had no problem with drugs or gambling.

Carol managed money poorly. I could never understand with all the money I made why we could never afford to buy a house. There were no savings.

Her strengths included being a good mother who kept the house clean and who was a good cook. Her weaknesses centered around being moody—would not talk for days at a time; self-righteous—always complaining about my drinking, which wasn't that much; insensitive—couldn't understand my need to go out with my friends.

Courtship:

We met in high school. I was physically attracted to her. Our dates were movies and visits to friends. We used to talk about everything. The only arguments we had were over her seeing other guys. I would catch her talking to them in the school hallways. We never had any temporary separations during the courtship.

We decided to marry when she became pregnant after we had been dating for about a half-year. I was going to ask her to marry me even before she became pregnant. This simply made me do it quicker than I had planned. Everyone thought it was a good idea for us to get married, especially when they heard she was expecting a baby.

Wedding and Honeymoon:

There were no problems on the night of the rehearsal or the day of the wedding, except when we went out to dinner her father and my mother had an argument over something. I can't remember what it was about. There was no honeymoon because we didn't have the money.

Married Life:

Carol took care of the inside chores while I took care of the outside chores. Both of us shared in caring for the children. We were good parents. There wasn't time together because I worked long hours in order to provide for my four children and my wife. She never enjoyed going out, so we didn't have much of a social life.

We used to argue about my drinking because she couldn't understand why I would stop off for a drink on the way home from work, or have a beer before going to bed. I didn't have a problem with alcohol and there never was any trouble with drugs. I do have a bad temper, but I never hit her or the kids. There were times when I broke things, in order to avoid hitting them.

She was not sensitive toward my sexual

needs. There was always an excuse for not having sex. Either she was too tired or the kids were around. Although I have no proof, I am sure she was fooling around with one of the neighbors. She always denied it. I was never unfaithful to her.

Neither her parents nor my parents interfered during the marriage. As I mentioned earlier, she was a poor money manager. She spent money constantly on expensive gifts for the kids and her family: shoes, coats, jewelry.

She used to tell me that she wanted us to go for counseling, but I could not see how a stranger could help us solve our problems.

Final Separation:

I was shocked when she took our daughter and left me. What happened was that my daughter and I had a little argument. Carol blew the argument out of proportion and used it as an excuse to leave. I tried to get her to come back or to go see someone, but she refused. If she had not gone to her friend's, Roberta Stowe, I think I could have convinced her to return. Roberta never liked me.

Present Status:

I am not married, nor do I have any immediate intention to do so. I still love Carol and wish we could get back together again. On occasions, I do date, but nothing serious.

I see my children on a regular basis. No child support is required. My life is going as well as can be expected.

Having not been in touch with Carol for the past two years, I really don't know what is happening in her life, other than what the kids tell me. I understand she is dating, but nothing serious. She is working her first full-time job at some law firm. That is all I know.

ROBERTA STOWE'S AFFIDAVIT

Carol's Background:

I have known Carol ever since grammar school and was her maid of honor. Her parents didn't have a good relationship because her father was an alcoholic, who physically abused her mother. In later years, Carol told me how her sisters, brother, and she used to hide in the cellar during these arguments, praying, asking God not to let their father kill their mother. She hated her father because of the way he treated the family. I am not aware of the father ever beating the kids, but he was verbally abusive often. Once, while visiting Carol, he called her every name in the book in front of me. While she hated her father, Carol got along well with her mother, brother, and sisters.

Carol wanted to attend college, but she married Thad soon after graduating from high school. She never worked during the marriage, other than a part-time job from time to time. She didn't have many friends either before or after the marriage, first because of her father, then because of Thad not wanting her to be around anyone other than himself. Thad was the only one that she dated.

Her goals were to be a good mother and wife. She attended Mass weekly and daily during the season of Lent. She never had a problem with alcohol or with drugs. She did a great job of managing their finances, considering the money that was wasted at the bar by Thad.

Carol is kind, sensitive, mature, and responsible. She has always been a bit moody, having her ups and downs. Making other people happy seemed to be another one of her goals. She always put herself second, was critical of herself, and often took the blame even when she didn't deserve it.

Thaddeus' Background:

I came to know Thad during high school, even before he started to date Carol. I really don't know much about his family background. Carol said his mother used to discipline the children with a belt and was a tough woman to get along with. Thad's father was a heavy drinker. I do not know how this affected the family. Thad was not close to either his mother or his father. He seldom spoke about either of them.

Thad was very close to his brother who used to, and still does, go drinking with Thad. During high school, they were like the local hoods, being bullies, getting into fights and beating up on other kids. They both had terrible tempers. Thad barely graduated from high school, then went to work for his father and is still working there.

Thad's circle of friends were all drinkers, being on the wild side. Carol was the only one he dated. His only goal in life was to have a good time. I never remember him attending any church.

He has been drinking alcohol ever since his sophomore year in high school. He followed in the footsteps of his father, becoming an alcoholic. The only difference between his father and Thad was that his father was a happy drunk, while Thad became mean and cruel. Thad never believed he had a problem and is still drinking heavily today.

As far as I know, other than smoking pot, there was no problem with drugs. I am not aware of him gambling, but he did spend money foolishly at the bars, buying rounds for everyone in the bar.

I think he was loyal to his friends, doing anything he could for them. He was a hard worker who never missed a day of work. He was jealous and possessive. He would not let Carol go anywhere without knowing exactly where she would be, with whom, and when she would be returning. If he disapproved of any of her friends, she was not allowed to see them again. He was also stubborn — everything had to be his way. He was selfish — always bought himself the best of everything. I don't remember him ever buying Carol a gift, not even an anniversary gift. He had a violent temper which I will describe later in the marriage section.

Courtship:

Carol and Thad met in school during their senior year. They dated on weekends. She seemed to worship the ground that he walked on, doing anything he told her to do. He told her what, when, and how to do things.

He lost his temper whenever she talked to another boy. Although he accused her of being unfaithful many times, she was never unfaithful. He called daily, checking on her. If she wasn't home when he called, he would show up at her house and wait on the steps until she came home, then he would put her through the third degree. She never asserted herself with him on any issues. He was free to do whatever he wanted and he did. He hung around with his friends whenever he wasn't around Carol. He could always be seen with a beer in his hand.

Theirs was a fast-moving courtship. After about seven or eight months of dating, Carol became pregnant and they decided to get married. I questioned her as to whether she wanted to be married to him for the rest of her life. She told me that she wanted her child to have a name and a good home. She loved Thad and believed he would change after marriage. Besides, he was better than her father. After her father discovered that she was pregnant, he never let up on the verbal abuse about how she brought so much shame upon the family. She really had no choice but to marry and to get out of the house.

Wedding and Honeymoon:

After the rehearsal, Thad proceeded to get drunk, falling asleep in his car. The best man had to wake him up, and almost had to carry Thad into the house. The day of the wedding was fine until the dinner. Thad's mother and Carol's father had an argument over something. I don't even remember what it was about, but everyone felt uncomfortable. They didn't go on a honeymoon.

Married Life:

He never shared in any of the household chores or in childcare. Carol didn't mind doing all the chores or caring for the children, except that he was critical of everything. Shortly after the marriage began, he started going out with his brother to the bars, staying out until the bars closed. I don't know how often he did this, but any time that I visited Carol or talked to her on the telephone, he was not there in the evening. I didn't mind this, because I was uncomfortable around him. I will explain why later. Carol and the children had no social life with Thad.

Although he was seldom around, he was the boss of the house without a doubt. No decision could be made without his final approval. If his opinion was different from Carol's, it would have to go his way.

Thad's drinking continued throughout the marriage, getting worse as time went on. Although there were days when he woke up on the front lawn from the night before, he never felt he had a drinking problem. He felt that Carol was seeing a problem where there was no problem.

I was not aware of any drug abuse.

There was physical violence during the marriage on the part of Thad. During a few visits, when Thad wasn't there, Carol showed me the holes behind the pictures. I don't know if he was physically abusive toward her early in the marriage, but in later years, I saw Carol with bruises on her arms. Once he gave her a black eye.

He was never physically abusive toward the children, but he was very critical of everything they did, using abusive and vulgar language. There was one exception to this. He punched his daughter and knocked her out at the end of the marriage. This was actually the cause of the final separation.

According to Carol, she never refused him sex, because if she tried, he would force himself upon her, so why bother refusing. She did not enjoy it with him because of the smell of the alcohol on his breath and his lack of sensitivity.

She was never unfaithful to him during the whole marriage, but he constantly accused her of this. I do not know whether he was, but once, when he was drunk, he did come on to me early in the marriage once after I had been babysitting while they went out. He said he was giving me the opportunity to enjoy what Carol enjoyed. From that time on, I was never comfortable around Thad.

Their families never interfered with the marriage. Carol and Thad did have financial problems because of the amount of money he spent at the bars. They never had any savings; therefore, they never had a house of their own.

Carol wanted him to go for counseling with her, but Thad said there was nothing wrong with the marriage.

Final Separation:

One evening Carol came to my door with her daughter, who had a swollen face and was crying hysterically. The daughter and

Thad had gotten into an argument, resulting in him knocking the daughter out with a punch to her face. Carol said she would never return to him. I thought to myself, "It's about time!" I allowed them to stay with me until they got established.

Present Status:

Carol has her own apartment and is working for a law firm. She has finally found the freedom to enjoy life. I understand that Thad has moved back with his parents and continues to drink heavily. The only time he sees the children is when they make the effort to see him.

In closing, the only reason this marriage continued as long as it did was Carol's commitment to the ideal of marriage as forever. If there are any other questions, please feel free to write or to call me.

THE TRIBUNAL'S EVALUATION

This chapter has presented the testimony of the petitioner (Carol Shield), the respondent (Thaddeus Jones, Carol's former husband), and one witness (Roberta Stowe, a lifelong friend of the petitioner).

In an actual annulment case two or more additional witnesses would likely be asked to provide further testimony regarding the marriage of Carol and Thaddeus. Their testimony may well corroborate some of the statements made by the petitioner and the respondent about the marriage and specific important events that transpired during the courtship, wedding, honeymoon, and period when the couple was married.

It is not at all unusual for the former husband and wife to see things differently. If they had agreed on more things, they might not be divorced and seeking an annulment. Still, there is no reason to doubt that everyone is truthfully telling, from his or her own point of view, what he or she remembers to have occurred.

The differences in the testimony present a bit of a problem for the tribunal staff who must sift through the many statements in order to determine as closely as possible the actual facts and conditions of the marriage. The tribunal staff can accomplish this more readily when the petitioner releases the tribunal from strict confidentiality so that a staff member can question the respondent about those particular instances where the testimony of the former spouses is in direct conflict.

The testimony presented in this chapter is similar to the testimony presented in numerous annulment petitions. On the basis of the written and oral marital history provided by the former husband and wife along with the statements of the witnesses, the judge of the tribunal determines whether an annulment should be granted or not.

8. How Can I Find Healing and Help to Begin Again?

The previous chapters are meant to help you prepare your annulment petition. They are filled with directions and information directed toward your intellect.

This chapter is aimed at your heart in an effort to help you heal some of the wounds and pain caused by your unhappy marriage and divorce. It will consider some of the common, painful issues faced by recently divorced Catholics, and offer some practical suggestions about resolving them.

Some of the suffering felt by a divorced person comes from the sense of guilt that arises when a divorce occurs. No matter how blameless you may be, there is often a feeling that you broke or violated your marriage vows in some way.

Divorced people are often plagued by the "what ifs." What if I had been more forgiving, prayed more, sought counseling sooner, and on and on.

As you look back at your marriage and its breakup, and examine the guilt you feel, try to objectively determine the actual degree of guilt. If the feeling of guilt is groundless, then it is time to let go of it, realizing that God understands it was beyond your control and ability to keep this commitment. If your feelings of guilt are based on actual fact and the result of things you did that harmed the marriage, then forgive yourself.

Remember that God forgives more often and more easily than people forgive others — especially themselves. Our God is known for being most loving and forgiving. If you are having difficulty forgiving yourself, speak with a priest or counselor who can help you experience the possibility of forgiveness.

After reading your marital history, you may ask, "How could I have made such a mistake and wasted so much time on this painful, pointless relationship?" It is important to realize it was not a mistake. With your background and the information you had about your former spouse, you made the right decision at the time. It is easy to be a "Monday morning quarterback" and see how yesterday's errors could have been prevented. It is much more difficult to see the errors as they are happening or before they occur. Accept the fact that you entered the marriage with the best of intentions based on the knowledge you had at the time. Now that you know better, don't beat yourself for past decisions. Applaud yourself for making the right decision to end the marriage and to begin your life anew.

If you have learned what you did right and what you did wrong in your first marriage, you can use that knowledge to establish a relationship with a more compatible partner. This deeper self-knowledge will enable you to enter into a valid sacramental marriage. If this happens, then your first marriage and all the pain of separation and divorce were not a total waste. You have become a stronger and wiser person because of what you suffered.

You may still be feeling much anger toward your former spouse and possibly his or her family and friends. This anger may be justified, but who is it hurting? You are probably experiencing the pain of your anger much more than the person toward whom it is directed. It is your stomach that turns every time you hear that person's name mentioned. You are the one who is tossing and turning at night, thinking about how wrong he or she was for you. The annulment process can be the point at which you let go of the anger and allow the grace of healing to touch your heart and soul.

The best way out of anger is through forgiveness. You might ask, "How is it possible to forgive after all that he or she has done to me, my children, and my family and friends?" Forgiveness may seem absurd until you realize that forgiveness brings peace to you. Forgiveness becomes reasonable when you realize four things.

1.   You are forgiving the person not because he or she asked to be forgiven or deserves to be forgiven but because you need to forgive in order to be healed.

2. When you forgive someone, you are not condoning what he or she has done. You are forgiving the person for having done something wrong.

3. The more deeply you have been hurt, the longer it may take to completely forgive the person. It may take many acts of forgiveness on your part to finally forgive, and even then you may not completely forget the pain that was inflicted.

4. It is not necessary for you to inform the person that he or she is forgiven, although you may do so if you wish.

The information in this book is intended to assist you in the process of obtaining an annulment. During this process you will spend many hours completing the necessary forms and meeting with witnesses, tribunal staff members, your parish priest, and others.

Similarly, these few pages about healing are intended only to open the door of your heart to forgiveness and healing. Plan to spend time pondering the simple thoughts in this chapter, and consider discussing your pain, guilt, hurt, anger, and your need for healing and hope with a dear friend, counselor, confessor, or parish priest, deacon, or pastoral associate.

You may also find that your parish, your diocese, or a local retreat center offers programs for people who are separated or divorced. These programs and similar support groups can be a source of great strength and a visible sign that you are not alone.

May God bless you with peace, healing, hope, and many good friends. If it be your heart's deepest desire, may your annulment free you to establish a permanent, loving, enriching, mature sacramental marriage.

Glossary

Affiant:

An affiant submits information with regard to the relationship between the petitioner and respondent through a written affidavit, rather than by oral testimony as a witness does.

Affidavit:

An affidavit is a written statement, signed by the author before a Notary Public. The Notary attests to the fact that the person appeared before him or her, and made an oath to the truthfulness of the statement.

Annulment:

An annulment is a declaration by the Catholic Church that a marriage is null and void. In essence, the Catholic Church decrees that a valid marriage never existed. Such a decision is made by the marriage tribunal of a diocese or archdiocese after gathering testimony from the former spouses and from affiants or witnesses.

Appellate Court:

The appellate court, ordinarily the second instance court, is the court of appeals. This court ratifies, overturns, or confirms the decision of the first instance court.

Canon Law:

Canon law is the body of rules governing the Catholic Church.

Competence:

Competence is the jurisdiction needed by a tribunal before it may consider a case.

Decree of Nullity:

A decree of nullity (often called an "annulment") is a document stating that a previous marriage bond is annulled. See "annulment."

Defender of the Bond:

The defender of the bond is the person who has the responsibility to point out and clarify any reasonable evidence in favor of the validity of the marriage being examined.

Expert:

In an annulment case, the expert is ordinarily a psychologist or psychiatrist who will give an opinion on the case from a psychological point of view.

First Instance Court:

The first instance court is the court in which the case receives its first hearing.

Guardian:

The tribunal assigns a guardian to a case to protect the rights of a respondent (former spouse) who for various reasons is not notified of the annulment proceedings that are taking place.

Invalid Marriage:

An invalid marriage is one in which some radical defect, present at the time of the marriage, rendered the marital consent ineffacious.

Judge:

The judge is the person from the marriage tribunal who renders a decision, based on canon law, on the validity (legality) or invalidity (nullity) of the marriage after hearing all the evidence.

Marital History:

The marital history is the account of the relationship between the petitioner and respondent as seen by the petitioner. The information in the marital history will include: the background of both parties, the courtship, rehearsal, wedding, reception, honeymoon, marriage relationship, final separation, and the present status of each party.

Petitioner:

The petitioner is the person who initiates the annulment case.

Premarital Investigation Book:

Premarital Investigation Book is a record book, usually containing the following information: the sacramental history of each of the parties and their responses to various questions regarding their freedom to marry, their understanding of the Catholic Church's rules for marriage, and their compliance with these rules. This book is retained by the church where the marriage took place and is referred to when an annulment petition is considered.

Preparator:

The member of the marriage tribunal staff who prepares the presentation of the case. This person can be a priest, religious Sister or Brother, or layperson who has the necessary training. This person's role is similar to that of a defense attorney in a civil case.

Prohibition:

The judge may place a prohibition on either the petitioner or respondent or both. A prohibition prevents the person from being married in a Catholic ceremony until the reason for the prohibition is removed.

This is done when the judge determines that the problems of one or both of the former spouses were the causes of the invalid marriage bond and that these problems may still be present. The removal of the prohibition is done by contacting the judge who placed it on the individual(s).

The judge will explain what is necessary to lift the prohibition, and then remove it when the conditions have been met.

Protocol Number:

A protocol number is usually assigned to a case as a means of identification.

Respondent:

The respondent is the former spouse of the petitioner.

Rota:

The Rota, the highest court of the Catholic Church, located in Vatican City, is ordinarily the third instance court. It is the final court of appeal in annulment cases.

Valid Marriage:

A valid marriage is the union of two people, entered into with the proper disposition and personality strengths as to make it possible for the couple to make a lifelong commitment to a loving union.

Witness:

A witness is a person who provides oral testimony during the annulment process regarding the relationship between the petitioner and the respondent. This is similar to the role of the affiant who also provides testimony. The difference is that the witness provides oral testimony while the affiant presents written testimony in an affidavit.

Annotated Bibliography

There are many helpful books on separation, divorce, and remarriage written from religious, legal, and psychological perspectives. Religious and secular bookstores as well as parish and public libraries have many books along with audio and video tapes on these topics. This list includes a few titles related directly to the topic of annulments.

Brunsman, Barry. *New Hope for Divorced Catholics.* San Francisco: HarperCollinsSanFrancisco, 1985.

> Information about divorce, remarriage, and annulment. Also explains how to form one's conscience and proceed when an annulment is not possible.

Code of Canon Law. Latin-English Edition. Washington, DC: Canon Law Society of America, 1983.

> The complete legal code for the Catholic Church, it details all the rules and regulations regarding the conditions for valid and sacramental marriages.

Tierney, Terence E. *Annulment: Do You Have a Case?* Revised and updated by Joseph J. Campo. Staten Island, NY: Alba House, 1994.

> Written in a practical style, it is intended help people understand the intricacies of the annulment procedure and determine if they have grounds to undertake the process.

United States Conference of Catholic Bishops. *Faithful to Each Other: A Catholic Handbook of Pastoral Help for Marriage Preparation.* Washington, DC: United States Catholic Conference, 1989.

> An excellent resource that offers the thoughts of the bishops of the United States on the importance of marriage and family life, along with practical suggestions for dealing with divorce and the annulment procedure.

Wrenn, Lawrence G. *Annulments.* Fifth Edition. Washington, DC: Canon Law Society of America, 1988.

> This book, along with companion books entitled *Decisions* and *Procedures*, while a bit technical, may provide additional information about the annulment process.

Zwack, Joseph P. *Annulment: Your Chance to Remarry Within the Catholic Church.* San Francisco: HarperCollins-SanFrancisco, 1983.

> In simple terms, this book explains the grounds and procedures by which people can have former marriages annulled by the Church.

About the Author

Ronald T. Smith, a Catholic priest of the Archdiocese of Hartford, studied at St. Thomas Seminary in Bloomfield, Connecticut; Mount Saint Mary Seminary in Emmittsburg, Maryland; and Hartford Seminary.

Ordained to the priesthood in 1973, he has served at parishes in Enfield, Hartford, and Bristol, Connecticut. In 1978 he began working at the Archdiocese of Hartford Marriage Tribunal as an instructor for marriage cases. In that capacity he has helped hundreds of divorced people understand, initiate, and complete the annulment procedure.

He is currently assigned as the chaplain for New Britain General Hospital and continues to work with the marriage tribunal and serve as an instructor for marriage cases.

ALSO OF INTEREST

KIDS ARE NONDIVORCEABLE: A Workbook for Divorced Parents and Their Children, Ages 6-11 by Sara Bonkowski. The ideal resource for parents seeking to help their children deal with issues surrounding separation and divorce. 128 pages, $7.95.

TEENS ARE NONDIVORCEABLE by Sara Bonkowski. This is the companion volume to *Kids Are Nondivorceable*, specifically written for parents with teenage children 12-18 years old. 160 pages, $7.95.

TOTS ARE NONDIVORCEABLE by Sara Bonkowski. The newest version of this series for parents of very young children from birth to 5 years of age. 112 pages, $8.95.

DIVORCE AND BEYOND by James Greteman and Leon Haverkamp. This support-group program for newly divorced persons focuses on the "mourning period" of the divorce process and concentrates mainly in the divorced persons themselves, rather than on their role as parents. Participant's Book, 132 pages, $5.95; Facilitator's Manual, 80 pages, $5.95.

TO TRUST AGAIN by William Urbine. A complete, self-contained program for marriage preparation for couples in which one or both parties have been involved in a previous marriage which ended through death or divorce. Couple's Workbook, 48 pages, $4.95; Leader's Guide, 48 pages, $9.95; Remarriage Inventory, 32 pages, $4.95.

DAILY MEDITATIONS (WITH SCRIPTURE) FOR BUSY MOMS by Patricia Robertson. Insightful, down-to-earth reflections for each day of the year paired with surprising and illuminating quotes from the Bible. 368 pages, $8.95.

DAILY MEDITATIONS (WITH SCRIPTURE) FOR BUSY DADS by Patrick T. Reardon. A companion to the Moms book just for Dads. 368 pages, $8.95.

Available at bookstores or by calling 800-397-2282.